Christmas treats

to make and give

Linda Collister

with photography by William Reavell

Christmas treats

to make and give

RYLAND
PETERS
& SMALL

LONDON NEW YORK

Senior Designer Toni Kay
Editor Céline Hughes
Production Gemma John
Art Director Leslie Harrington
Publishing Director Alison Starling

Food Stylist Rachel Miles
Prop Stylist Liz Belton
Indexer Hilary Bird

First published in the UK in 2008
by Ryland Peters & Small
20–21 Jockey's Fields
London WC1R 4BW
www.rylandpeters.com

10 9 8 7 6 5 4 3 2 1

Text © Linda Collister 2008
Design and photographs
© Ryland Peters & Small 2008

All photography by William Reavell,
except pages 21, 29, 34 and 73 by
Diana Miller.

Printed in China

ISBN: 978 1 84597 719 1

A CIP record for this book is
available from the British Library.

Author's acknowledgements
I would like to thank the following
for their help: Barbara Levy, Céline
Hughes, William Reavell, Toni Kay,
Liz Belton, Rachel Miles, and Stevie
and Dan Hertz.

Notes
• All spoon measurements are
level, unless otherwise specified.
• All eggs are medium, unless
otherwise specified. It is generally
recommended that free-range eggs
be used. Uncooked or partly cooked
eggs should not be served to the
very young, the very old, those with
compromised immune systems, or
to pregnant women.
• Ovens should be preheated to the
specified temperature. Recipes in
this book were tested using a regular
oven. If using fan-assisted, follow
the manufacturer's instructions for
adjusting temperatures.
• To sterilize preserving jars, wash
them in hot, soapy water and rinse
in boiling water. Place in a large
pan, then cover with hot water.
With the lid on, bring the water to
the boil and continue boiling for
15 minutes. Turn off the heat, then
leave the jars in the hot water until
just before they are to be filled.
Sterilize the lids for 5 minutes. Jars
should be filled and sealed while
they are still hot.

Contents

introduction   6

little bakes   10

brownies, bars and cakes 42

savoury treats   70

preserves   84

suppliers   94

index   95

Introduction

In our house, you *smell* Christmas first: the warm, spicy sweetness of festive baking, the fresh green-ness of newly cut pine. And the celebrations begin as we prepare to make edible gifts and treats. Many families develop their own traditions and make the same favourites every year. But ours is a family of different residences, nationalities, backgrounds and interests, so each year we try something new.

The easiest recipes in this book – the decorated biscuits and cookies – are also the most impressive. These are based on the crisp, gently spiced and fragrant biscuits popular in Advent markets across northern Europe for many centuries. Supermarkets and kitchen shops sell the tools you'll need, and these make great stocking fillers. You can buy fancy cutters in seasonal shapes, writing icing pens, edible decorations, ribbons and threads for hanging. Children love to be involved, so wrap them in aprons and get them into the kitchen. If you don't want to put the finished biscuits on the tree itself (they're miniature works of art after all!), you can hang them elsewhere: from ropes of tinsel, stripped twigs, thin copper pipes or wooden rods. Another easy project, suitable for children, is the Truffles (page 68): they are not too rich and are good gifts for teachers.

The more sophisticated biscuits – the German Lebkuchen (page 19), French Chocolate Fingers (page 31), Dutch Vanilla Butter Biscuits (page 23) – also make good presents. Pack them into pretty boxes or tins (my children cover old coffee tins in wrapping paper) or wrap them in cellophane and lots of coloured ribbon. Label them with storage instructions, a list of ingredients in case of allergies and the 'eat-by' date (the recipes will give you all the information you need).

With a bit of forward planning, you can get ahead with festive meals. I make a big batch of Cranberry and Basil Relish (page 87) to go with our Thanksgiving turkey and keep a jar for Christmas, when we have another turkey with all the traditional and well-loved trimmings. Like the Ginger Fruit Relish (page 88), it is also good for livening up the leftovers, the cold meats, ham and cheese served in our house from Boxing Day until New Year or until the turkey is no more.

On Christmas day itself I serve a selection of savoury nibbles to soak up the pre-lunch Champagne. These can be made ahead, frozen, then warmed before serving – try the Chilli Cheese Gougères (page 76) or some rich and crumbly Cheese Palmiers (page 75). Any leftovers are good served with soup. The Grissini (page 80) are breadsticks served with dips or wrapped in Parma ham or prosciutto. The easiest possible recipes are also the most irresistible – Spicy Nuts and Marinated Olives (both page 83).

It's fun when friends and family drop by unexpectedly to deliver cards and presents, but I've often been caught on the hop. So I've learnt to prepare and hide a stash of home-made cakes that double as dessert. I now appreciate why my grandmother, born into a big family in the nineteenth century, said she could face the festivities as long as she had a ham, a matured cheese and a large fruitcake in the larder. Brownies (pages 44–47) are always a winner and can be transformed into an easy dessert if served warm with ice cream and a drizzle of melted chocolate. A cut-and-come-again cake such as the Lemon Pecan (page 56) or the quick and simple Chocolate Brandy (page 52) will be popular with everyone. But for sheer versatility muffins (pages 60–65) are wonderful – for breakfasts and brunches, mid-afternoon snacks and midnight feasts – and they can be made in advance and kept in the freezer. Meanwhile, for an indulgent New Year's Day breakfast, try some little Brioches (page 59).

Start baking and bring the fun and fragrance of Christmas into your house!

Little
bakes

GOOD TO EAT AND FUN TO DECORATE, THEN HANG FROM FINE RED OR SILVER RIBBONS. TRY DECORATING WITH GLACÉ ICING MADE FROM SIEVED ICING SUGAR MIXED WITH A LITTLE CLEAR HONEY RATHER THAN WATER.

Iced honey and cinnamon biscuits

300 g plain flour
2 teaspoons ground cinnamon
1 teaspoon ground mixed spice
175 g unsalted butter, chilled and diced
6 tablespoons honey

To decorate

royal or glacé icing, or writing icing pens, silver balls, thin ribbon (see Suppliers, page 94)

shaped biscuit cutters
several baking trays, lightly greased

MAKES ABOUT 24, DEPENDING ON SIZE OF CUTTERS

Put the flour, cinnamon and mixed spice into the bowl of a food processor. Pulse a couple of times just to mix. Add the diced butter and process until the mixture looks like fine crumbs. Add the honey and process until the mixture comes together to make a soft dough.

Remove the dough from the bowl, shape into a ball and wrap in clingfilm. Chill until firm, about 30 minutes. The dough can be kept in the fridge, tightly wrapped, for up to 5 days.

Remove the dough from the fridge, unwrap and roll out on a lightly floured work surface until about 5 mm thick. Dip the biscuit cutters in flour and cut out shapes from the dough. Gather up the trimmings and re-roll, then cut more shapes. Arrange the shapes slightly apart on the prepared baking trays. If using as decorations, use a skewer or cocktail stick to make a small hole at the top of each shape large enough to thread a ribbon through. Chill for 10–15 minutes until firm.

Preheat the oven to 180°C (350°F) Gas 4.

Bake in the preheated oven for 10–12 minutes until just firm. Leave to cool for 3 minutes on the trays, then transfer to a wire rack until completely cold. Decorate with royal icing (page 15) or glacé icing (page 16), or use a writing icing pen. Add silver balls while the icing is wet, but wait until the icing is thoroughly dry before threading with ribbon. Store the biscuits in an airtight container and eat within 5 days.

LIGHTLY GOLDEN AND WELL SPICED, THESE ARE RICHER THAN THE USUAL GINGERBREAD MEN, BUT FOR A DEEPER COLOUR REPLACE THE LIGHT MUSCOVADO SUGAR WITH DARK MUSCOVADO.

Gingerbread shapes

350 g plain flour
1 tablespoon ground ginger
1 teaspoon bicarbonate of soda
1 teaspoon ground cinnamon
175 g unsalted butter
150 g light muscovado sugar
4 tablespoons golden syrup

To decorate
royal or glacé icing, or writing icing pens, ribbons, edible silver balls (see Suppliers, page 94)

shaped biscuit cutters
several baking trays,
lined with non-stick baking paper

MAKES ABOUT 18 MEDIUM OR 12 LARGE

Sift the flour, ginger, bicarbonate of soda and cinnamon into a bowl.

Put the butter, sugar and golden syrup into a pan large enough to hold all the ingredients. Set over low heat to melt very gently. Remove the pan from the heat and add all the sieved ingredients. Mix thoroughly with a wooden spoon to make a firm dough. Leave until cool enough to handle. Turn out onto a work surface and knead gently to make a neat ball, then wrap in clingfilm and chill until firm, about 20 minutes.

Preheat the oven to 180°C (350°F) Gas 4.

Remove the dough from the fridge, unwrap and roll out on a lightly floured work surface until 5 mm thick. Dip the biscuit cutters in flour and cut out shapes. Gather up the trimmings and re-roll, then cut out more shapes. Arrange slightly apart on the prepared trays. Bake in the oven for 8–10 minutes until lightly browned. If using as decorations, use a skewer or cocktail stick to make a small hole at the top of each shape large enough to thread a ribbon through. Leave to cool completely, then decorate with royal icing (see below) or glacé icing (page 16), or use a writing icing pen. Add silver balls while the icing is wet, but wait until the icing is thoroughly dry before threading with ribbon. Store the shapes in an airtight container and eat within 1 week.

Royal icing – This can be coloured with a few drops of icing food colouring and hardens as it dries. It is easily piped using a greaseproof paper icing bag with a fine writing tip or with the tip of the bag snipped off. Sift 200 g icing sugar into a bowl and stir in an egg white to make an icing that is stiff but can be piped or spread. Spoon into the icing bag and snip off the point when ready to decorate.

THESE WELL-FLAVOURED BISCUITS ARE SIMPLE TO
MAKE AND ARE IDEAL DECORATIONS. PICK YOUR
FAVOURITE BISCUIT CUTTERS, THEN ONCE THEY ARE
BAKED, HAVE FUN ICING AND FINISHING.

Iced star biscuits

150 g unsalted butter,
at room temperature

100 g caster sugar

finely grated zest and
freshly squeezed juice of
1 unwaxed lemon

75 g cream cheese

300 g plain flour

a good pinch of salt

1 teaspoon ground mixed spice

To decorate

royal or glacé icing, or writing
icing pens, edible silver balls,
ribbons (see Suppliers, page 94)

a star-shaped biscuit cutter

several baking trays

MAKES ABOUT 24
10-CM STARS

Beat the butter with the sugar and lemon zest using a wooden spoon
or electric mixer. Beat in 2 teaspoons of the lemon juice and all the
cream cheese. Sift in the flour, salt and mixed spice and work in.
When thoroughly combined, remove the dough from the bowl, shape
into a ball and wrap in clingfilm. Chill until firm, about 30 minutes.
The dough can be kept in the fridge, tightly wrapped, for up to 1 week.

Preheat the oven to 180°C (350°F) Gas 4.

Remove the dough from the fridge, unwrap and roll out on a lightly
floured work surface until 5 mm thick. Dip the biscuit cutter in flour
and cut out shapes. Gather up the trimmings and re-roll, then cut out
more shapes. Arrange slightly apart on the baking trays. If using as
decorations, use a skewer or cocktail stick to make a small hole at the
top of each shape large enough to thread a ribbon through. Bake for
12–15 minutes until just turning golden brown at the edges. Remove
from the oven, leave to cool for 3 minutes, then transfer to a wire
rack until completely cold. Decorate with royal icing (page 15) or
glacé icing (see below), or use a writing icing pen. When firm, thread
with ribbons. Store in an airtight container and eat within 5 days.

Glacé icing – Made with icing sugar and water, plus a little colouring if
you like. It will dry firm but not as hard as royal icing. Sift 100 g icing
sugar into a bowl. Stir in water or lemon juice, a teaspoon at a time,
to make a thick icing that can be piped. If you want to spread the
icing, add a little more water to make a consistency that runs slowly
off the back of the wooden spoon when it is held up above the bowl.

IN GERMANY, IT WOULDN'T BE CHRISTMAS WITHOUT LEBKUCHEN. FOLLOWING A TRADITION THAT DATES BACK TO THE MEDIEVAL MONASTERIES, THEY ARE MADE FROM HONEY AND SEVEN SPICES TO REPRESENT THE SEVEN DAYS OF GOD'S CREATION. THIS IS MY FAVOURITE VERSION, BASED ON MERINGUE AND NUTS AND WITH JUST SIX SPICES — CRISP AND LIGHT BUT DENSELY FLAVOURED.

Lebkuchen

100 g almonds (not blanched)

25 g dark chocolate, coarsely chopped

2 tablespoons mixed peel, very finely chopped

½ teaspoon ground cinnamon

½ teaspoon ground ginger

¼ teaspoon freshly grated nutmeg

¼ teaspoon ground black pepper

¼ teaspoon ground cloves

¼ teaspoon ground allspice

2 large egg whites

115 g icing sugar, sifted

To decorate

150 g good dark chocolate, chopped

several baking trays, lined with non-stick baking paper

MAKES 16

Preheat the oven to 150°C (300°F) Gas 2.

Put the almonds and chopped chocolate into the bowl of a food processor and process until the mixture looks like fine crumbs. Mix with the finely chopped peel and all the spices.

Put the egg whites into a spotlessly clean, grease-free bowl and, using an electric whisk or mixer, whisk until stiff peaks form. Gradually whisk in the icing sugar, then whisk for another minute to make a very stiff, glossy meringue. Sprinkle the spice mixture over the top and gently fold in with a large metal spoon.

Take tablespoons of the mixture and drop them on the prepared baking trays, spacing them well apart to allow for spreading. Using a round-bladed knife, spread out each mound to a disc about 7 cm across. Bake in the preheated oven for 15–20 minutes, until pale gold and firm.

Remove the trays from the oven, set on a wire rack and leave to cool completely. When cold, peel the lebkuchen off the baking paper.

To decorate, melt the chocolate in a heatproof bowl set over a pan of steaming but not boiling water. Do not let the base of the bowl touch the water. Stir gently until melted, then remove from the heat. Spread some melted chocolate over one side of each lebkuchen with a palette knife, then leave to set on a sheet of non-stick baking paper.

Store in an airtight container and eat within 4 days.

TRADITIONALLY MADE FOR THE CHRISTMAS
HOLIDAYS, THESE DARK SPICY BISCUITS CAN BE LEFT
PLAIN OR DECORATED WITH WHITE ICING – YOU CAN
USE READY-MADE ICING WRITING PENS FOR THIS.

Swedish pepper biscuits

200 g plain flour

½ teaspoon bicarbonate of soda

1 teaspoon ground cinnamon

1 teaspoon ground ginger

½ teaspoon ground black pepper

freshly grated zest of
1 unwaxed orange

150 g caster sugar

115 g unsalted butter,
chilled and diced

1 egg, lightly beaten

1 tablespoon black treacle

a star-shaped biscuit cutter

several baking trays, greased

MAKES ABOUT 15

Put all the ingredients in a food processor and blend until the mixture forms a soft dough.

When thoroughly combined, remove the dough from the processor, shape into a ball and wrap in clingfilm. Chill until firm, about 1 hour.

Remove the dough from the fridge, unwrap and roll out on a lightly floured work surface until about 5 mm thick. Dip the biscuit cutter in flour and cut out shapes. Gather up the trimmings and re-roll, then cut out more shapes. Arrange the biscuits slightly apart on the prepared baking trays and chill for 10 minutes.

Preheat the oven to 160°C (325°F) Gas 3.

Bake in the preheated oven for 10–12 minutes until dark golden brown and firm.

Leave to cool for 5 minutes, then transfer to a wire rack until completely cold. Store in an airtight container and eat within 1 week or freeze for up to 1 month.

THESE ARE RICHER THAN SHORTBREAD YET EASY TO MAKE (THERE'S NO
ROLLING AND CUTTING) AND FLAVOURED WITH VANILLA POD SEEDS. IF YOU
PREFER YOU CAN USE A TEASPOON OF REALLY GOOD VANILLA EXTRACT. THE
DOUGH CAN BE STORED IN AN AIRTIGHT CONTAINER IN THE FRIDGE FOR UP
TO 5 DAYS BEFORE BAKING.

Dutch vanilla butter biscuits

225 g unsalted butter,
at room temperature

175 g caster sugar

1 vanilla pod, about 8 cm

1 large egg

250 g plain flour

½ teaspoon baking powder

a good pinch of salt

demerara or raw cane sugar,
to decorate

several baking trays

MAKES ABOUT 24

Preheat the oven to 180°C (350°F) Gas 4.

Put the butter and sugar into the bowl of a food processor. Split the
vanilla pod lengthways, scrape out the tiny black seeds with the tip of
a knife and add them to the bowl. Beat until light and creamy. Beat in
the egg, beating until very light and fluffy.

Sift the flour, baking powder and salt into the bowl and mix in using
the lowest possible speed.

Flour your hands, then take a walnut-sized piece of dough and roll it
into a ball. Set on a baking tray. Repeat with the rest of the dough,
arranging the biscuits well apart to allow for spreading. Lightly sprinkle
the tops with sugar – there's no need to flatten the biscuits – then bake
in the preheated oven for 15–18 minutes until lightly golden and
slightly darker around the edges.

Leave the biscuits to cool on the baking trays for 2 minutes, then
transfer to a wire rack until completely cold. Store in an airtight
container and eat within 5 days or freeze for up to 1 month.

THIS RECIPE WAS VERY POPULAR WHEN I WAS SMALL AND
PEANUT BUTTER WAS CONSIDERED RATHER EXOTIC – MY
FATHER BROUGHT OUR FIRST JAR HOME AS A TREAT FROM
A TRIP TO CHICAGO – BUT I'VE ADDED THE CHUNKS OF
LOVELY BITTER, DARK CHOCOLATE AS I LIKE THE CONTRAST
TO THE SALTY SWEETNESS OF THE COOKIE MIX. LOOK OUT
FOR THE BEST QUALITY UNSWEETENED PEANUT BUTTER.

Peanut butter choc chunkies

275 g crunchy peanut butter
175 g light muscovado sugar
½ teaspoon vanilla extract
1 large egg, beaten
50 g plain flour
100 g good dark chocolate,
coarsely chopped

*several baking trays,
lined with non-stick baking paper*

MAKES 24

Preheat the oven to 180°C (350°F) Gas 4.

Put the peanut butter, sugar, vanilla extract and egg into a mixing
bowl and mix thoroughly with a wooden spoon. Work in the flour
and the chocolate, then use your hands to bring the dough together
– it will be a bit crumbly.

Take a tablespoon of dough and roll it into a ball. Set on a prepared
baking tray. Repeat with the rest of the dough, arranging the
chunkies well apart to allow for spreading, then slightly flatten with
the back of a fork. Bake in the preheated oven for 12–15 minutes
until just firm and golden and slightly coloured around the edges.

Remove the trays from the oven and set on a wire rack to cool
completely. Lift the cold chunkies off the tray and store in an
airtight container. Best eaten within 1 week.

POSSIBLY THE WORLD'S RICHEST CHOCOLATE
COOKIE, MADE WITH AN AWFUL LOT OF GOOD DARK
CHOCOLATE (BOTH MELTED AND IN CHUNKS MIXED
IN WITH WALNUTS), PLUS JUST A LITTLE FLOUR,
THEN DECORATED WITH MORE DARK CHOCOLATE.

Triple chocolate cookies

300 g dark chocolate,
coarsely chopped

55 g unsalted butter,
at room temperature

2 large eggs,
at room temperature

140 g caster sugar

½ teaspoon vanilla extract

3 tablespoons plain flour

¼ teaspoon baking powder

100 g walnut pieces

To decorate

50 g dark chocolate,
coarsely chopped

*several baking trays,
lined with non-stick baking paper*

MAKES 24

Preheat the oven to 180°C (350°F) Gas 4.

Put 200 g of the chopped dark chocolate in a heatproof bowl set
over a pan of steaming but not boiling water. Do not let the base
of the bowl touch the water. Stir gently until melted, then remove
from the heat. Gently stir in the butter.

Put the eggs, sugar and vanilla extract into the bowl of an electric
mixer and whisk until very thick and mousse-like and the whisk
leaves a ribbon-like trail when lifted – this will take 3–4 minutes.

Sift the flour and baking powder into the bowl and gently fold in
with a large metal spoon. Add the melted chocolate mixture and
fold in. When almost combined add the remaining 100 g chopped
dark chocolate and the walnut pieces and mix in.

Take tablespoons of the mixture and drop them on the prepared
baking trays, spacing them well apart to allow for spreading. Bake
in the preheated oven for 10 minutes until barely set.

Remove from the oven and set the trays on a wire rack until the
cookies have cooled completely.

To decorate, melt the chocolate in a heatproof bowl set over a
pan of steaming water (as above). Dip a fork or teaspoon into the
chocolate and drizzle over the cookies. Leave to set, then store
in an airtight container and eat within 1 week.

THESE SWEET, ALMOND-RICH BISCUITS ARE LIKE SOFT, CHEWY AMARETTI. SERVE WITH COFFEE AT THE END OF A SPECIAL MEAL; A BOX OF THEM MAKES A LOVELY GIFT.

Sardinian almond biscuits

450 g almond paste
100 g flaked almonds
2 egg whites
50 g icing sugar

*several baking trays,
lined with non-stick baking paper*

MAKES 30

Preheat the oven to 150°C (300°F) Gas 3.

Break up the almond paste and put in a food processor. Process briefly until the paste is finely chopped. Add 70 g of the almonds, the egg whites and sugar and process until the mixture forms a thick, smooth paste.

Take tablespoons of the mixture and drop them on the prepared baking trays, spacing them well apart to allow for spreading. Scatter the remaining almonds over the top. Bake in the preheated oven for about 25 minutes until light golden brown.

Remove from the oven and leave to cool completely on the trays. Store in an airtight container and eat within 1 week. These biscuits don't freeze very well.

Variation – Replace the almonds (in the mixture and for sprinkling) with pine nuts.

HERE ARE SOME ELEGANT PIPED CHOCOLATE BISCUITS,
FINISHED WITH DARK CHOCOLATE, THAT REALLY DO
MELT IN THE MOUTH. PIPING BAGS AND NOZZLES ARE
AVAILABLE FROM KITCHEN SHOPS AND THE BAKEWARE
DEPARTMENTS OF LARGE DEPARTMENT STORES, AS WELL
AS ONLINE (SEE SUPPLIERS, PAGE 94), AND CAN BE USED
TO PIPE MERINGUES, WHIPPED CREAM AND BISCUITS.

French chocolate fingers

175 g unsalted butter,
at room temperature

50 g caster sugar

½ teaspoon vanilla extract

25 g unsweetened cocoa powder

150 g plain flour

½ teaspoon baking powder

To decorate

75 g dark or white chocolate,
coarsely chopped

*a piping bag,
fitted with a fluted nozzle*

*several baking trays,
lined with non-stick baking paper*

MAKES ABOUT 30

Preheat the oven to 180°C (350°F) Gas 4.

Put the butter, sugar and vanilla extract into a bowl and beat with
a wooden spoon or electric mixer until light and fluffy. Sift in the
cocoa, flour and baking powder and fold in until thoroughly combined.

Spoon the mixture into the piping bag. Pipe the mixture onto the
prepared baking trays in fingers about 9 cm long, spacing them well
apart to allow for spreading. Bake in the preheated oven for about
15 minutes or until slightly coloured around the edges.

Remove from the oven and leave to cool completely on the trays – the
biscuits are quite fragile.

To decorate, melt the chocolate in a heatproof bowl set over a pan of
steaming but not boiling water. Do not let the base of the bowl touch
the water. Dip a fork or teaspoon into the chocolate and drizzle over
the cold biscuits. Leave to set, then store in an airtight container
and eat within 5 days.

VERY GLAMOROUS INDEED — THESE ULTRA CRISP SNAPS ARE LOVELY WITH COFFEE, ICE CREAM OR SORBET. BUT THE BEST WAY TO SERVE THEM IS TO DIP THE ENDS IN DARK CHOCOLATE THEN FILL THEM WITH WHIPPED, BRANDY-LACED CREAM.

Lacy brandy snaps

85 g unsalted butter

85 g caster sugar

3 tablespoons golden syrup

85 g plain flour

1 teaspoon ground ginger

2 teaspoons brandy

several baking trays, lined with non-stick baking paper

several wooden or stainless steel spoons with thick handles

MAKES 20

Preheat the oven to 180°C (350°F) Gas 4.

Put the butter, sugar and syrup in a small pan and set over gentle heat. Stir with a wooden spoon until melted and smooth. Remove the pan from the heat. Mix the flour with the ginger and stir into the melted mixture along with the brandy to make a smooth and thick batter.

Take tablespoons of the mixture and drop onto the prepared baking trays, spacing the snaps about 10 cm apart to allow for spreading (there is no need to spread out the mixture). Do not put more than 5 snaps on each tray. Bake 1 tray at a time in the preheated oven until bubbly and golden brown, 7–10 minutes.

Remove the tray from the oven and leave to cool for exactly 1 minute, then quickly lift each snap off the tray with a palette knife or spatula and gently roll around thick wooden or stainless steel spoon handles (I use a ladle) to make a hollow roll. The roll will firm up rapidly as it cools so you need to work quickly while it is warm and pliable. If the mixture has set before it can be shaped, return the tray to the oven for 1 minute until pliable again.

Leave the rolls to cool on the spoon handles until they are firm enough to hold their shape, then gently slide off, set on a wire rack and leave to cool completely. While the first batch is cooling, bake the second and so on. Store in an airtight container and eat within 1 week.

Brandy snap baskets – drape the warm snaps over small oranges to form cup shapes. Leave until set and firm, then lift off and turn the right way up. Fill, just before serving, with ice cream.

THIS RECIPE FOR SNOWY-WHITE, RICH ALMOND BISCUITS COMES FROM A CZECH FRIEND, BUT I'VE EATEN POLISH, GERMAN AND DUTCH VERSIONS, AND MY MOTHER-IN-LAW MAKES SOMETHING SIMILAR DURING HANNUKAH.

Czech almond crescents

125 g blanched almonds

60 g icing sugar, plus extra to dust

115 g unsalted butter, chilled and diced

2–3 drops real almond extract

100 g plain flour

several baking trays, well greased

MAKES 24

Put the almonds and sugar in a food processor and blend until the mixture becomes a fine, sandy powder. Add the butter, almond extract and flour and process until the mixture forms a ball of smooth dough.

Carefully remove the dough from the machine, wrap in clingfilm and chill for about 20 minutes or until firm. The dough can be kept in the fridge, tightly wrapped, for 24 hours.

When ready to cook, preheat the oven to 160°C (325°F) Gas 3.

Remove the dough from the fridge, unwrap and pull off a heaped teaspoon of the dough. Roll it with your hands to make a sausage shape about 7 cm long. Curve the dough into a crescent and set on a prepared baking tray. Repeat with the rest of the dough, arranging the crescents well apart on the trays. Bake in the preheated oven for 15–18 minutes until the edges are barely coloured.

Leave to cool on the trays for 2 minutes, then carefully transfer to a wire rack to cool completely. Just before serving, dust with plenty of icing sugar. Store in an airtight container and eat within 1 week. These biscuits are fragile and, while they can be frozen, they tend to break easily.

Variation – Melt 50 g good-quality dark chocolate and dip one end of each cooled crescent into the chocolate. Leave to set on non-stick baking paper. Sprinkle the plain end with icing sugar before serving.

SABLÉS ARE TO THE FRENCH WHAT SHORTBREAD IS TO SCOTS — MADE
FROM THE BEST BUTTER WITH A LIGHT HAND, AND JUST AS WELL
LOVED. THESE ARE STUDDED WITH PISTACHIOS ALTHOUGH YOU COULD
ALSO USE FINELY CHOPPED LIGHTLY TOASTED PECANS OR ALMONDS,
AND CUT INTO SIMPLE DISCS OR FANCY SHAPES AS YOU LIKE.

Pistachio sablés

115 g unsalted butter,
at room temperature

½ teaspoon vanilla extract

75 g icing sugar, sifted

1 large egg yolk

150 g plain flour

a good pinch of baking powder

a good pinch of salt

100 g shelled pistachios,
finely chopped

demerara or raw cane sugar,
to sprinkle

shaped biscuit cutters

*several baking trays,
lined with non-stick baking paper*

MAKES ABOUT 24

Beat together the butter, vanilla extract and icing sugar with an electric mixer (starting on low speed) or a wooden spoon. When the mixture is very light and fluffy, beat in the egg yolk.

Sift the flour, baking powder and salt into the bowl and work in with a wooden spoon. When almost combined, add the nuts and work in well.

Remove the dough from the bowl, shape into a ball and wrap in clingfilm. Chill until firm, about 15 minutes. The dough can be kept in the fridge, tightly wrapped, for up to 3 days.

When ready to cook, preheat the oven to 170°C (325°F) Gas 3.

Remove the dough from the fridge, unwrap and roll out on a lightly floured work surface until about 5 mm thick. Dip the biscuit cutters in flour and cut out shapes. Gather up the trimmings and re-roll, then cut out more shapes. Arrange slightly apart on the prepared baking trays and sprinkle with a little demerara or raw cane sugar. Bake in the preheated oven for 17–20 minutes until barely coloured and lightly golden around the edges.

Remove the trays from the oven and set on a wire rack. Leave to cool for 5 minutes until firm enough to transfer to a cooling rack. Store in an airtight container and eat within 1 week or freeze for up to 1 month.

EXCELLENT FOR DUNKING IN COFFEE OR A GLASS OF VIN SANTO, THESE CRISP, NUTTY BISCOTTI ARE GIVEN A FESTIVE TWIST WITH GOOD-QUALITY, SOFT-DRIED CRANBERRIES – LOOK OUT FOR THE TYPE DUSTED WITH GROUND CINNAMON FOR THE BEST FLAVOUR (OR ADD ½ TEASPOON GROUND CINNAMON WITH THE FLOUR).

Almond biscotti

115 g unsalted butter, at room temperature

125 g caster sugar

1 teaspoon vanilla extract

2 large eggs, at room temperature, beaten

275 g plain flour

a good pinch of salt

½ teaspoon baking powder

100 g ready-to-eat, soft-dried cranberries

150 g blanched almonds, roughly chopped

2 baking trays, lined with non-stick baking paper

MAKES 24

Preheat the oven to 180°C (350°F) Gas 4.

Beat together the butter, sugar and vanilla extract with an electric mixer or wooden spoon, until light and fluffy. Gradually beat in the eggs.

Sift the flour, salt and baking powder into the bowl and work in with a wooden spoon. When almost combined, add the cranberries and almonds and mix thoroughly to make a soft dough.

Turn out the dough onto a floured work surface and divide into 2 equal portions. Using well floured hands, lift a portion of dough onto each prepared baking tray and shape into a brick 26 x 9 cm. Bake in the preheated oven for about 25 minutes until golden and just firm.

Remove the trays from the oven, set on a wire rack and leave to cool for 10 minutes. Using a serrated bread knife, slice the logs (still on the trays) on the diagonal about 1 cm thick. Put, cut-side down, on the trays and return to the oven. Bake for 10 minutes until starting to colour.

Remove the trays from the oven, put on a wire rack and leave to cool completely. Store in an airtight container and eat within 3 weeks.

CRISP, CRUNCHY CHOCOLATE BISCUITS STUDDED WITH
CHUNKS OF DARK CHOCOLATE AND PECANS – LOVELY WITH
ICE CREAM AS WELL AS HOT DRINKS.

Chocolate chip biscotti

3 large eggs,
at room temperature

200 g light muscovado sugar

finely grated zest of
1 unwaxed orange

115 g unsalted butter, melted

325 g plain flour

1 tablespoon baking powder

25 g unsweetened cocoa powder

100 g pecan pieces

100 g dark chocolate,
coarsely chopped

*2 baking trays,
lined with non-stick baking paper*

MAKES ABOUT 36

Preheat the oven to 180°C (350°F) Gas 4.

Put the eggs, sugar and orange zest in the bowl of an electric mixer and whisk until very frothy. Whisk in the melted butter.

Sift the flour, baking powder and cocoa into the bowl and mix with a wooden spoon. Work in the pecans and chopped chocolate.

When thoroughly combined, turn out the dough onto a floured work surface and divide into 2 equal portions. Using well floured hands, lift a portion of dough onto each prepared tray and shape into a brick 30 x 7 cm – they will spread in the oven. Bake in the preheated oven for 25–30 minutes until just firm when pressed.

Remove the trays from the oven (you can turn off the oven) and leave to cool completely.

When ready to continue, reheat the oven to 180°C (350°F) Gas 4. Using a serrated bread knife, slice the logs (still on the trays) on the diagonal about 1 cm thick. Put, cut-side down, on the trays and return to the oven. Bake for 10 minutes until crisp and dry.

Remove the trays from the oven, put on a wire rack and leave to cool completely. Store in an airtight container and eat within 3 weeks.

Brownies, bars and cakes

THERE ARE NO NUTS BUT PLENTY OF CHOCOLATE
IN THESE MOIST, RICH BROWNIES. FOR THE MOST
INTENSE FLAVOUR, USE TOP-QUALITY WHITE AND
DARK CHOCOLATE.

Triple chocolate brownies

200 g dark chocolate,
coarsely chopped

100 g unsalted butter,
at room temperature, cubed

225 g caster sugar

½ teaspoon vanilla extract

4 large eggs,
at room temperature

60 g plain flour

60 g unsweetened cocoa powder

100 g white chocolate,
coarsely chopped

*a 25.5 x 20.5-cm baking tin,
greased and base-lined with
greaseproof paper*

MAKES 24

Preheat the oven to 180°C (350°F) Gas 4.

Melt the chocolate in a heatproof bowl set over a pan of steaming but not boiling water. Do not let the base of the bowl touch the water. Stir occasionally until melted, then remove the bowl from the heat and leave to cool until needed.

Beat the butter, sugar and vanilla extract with an electric mixer or wooden spoon until light and fluffy, then gradually beat in the eggs, beating well after each addition.

Stir in the melted chocolate, then sift the flour and cocoa into the bowl and mix in.

Transfer the mixture to the prepared tin and spread evenly. Scatter the chopped white chocolate over the top, then bake in the preheated oven for 20 minutes, or until a cocktail stick or skewer inserted halfway between the sides and the centre comes out slightly moist but not sticky with uncooked batter.

Remove the tin from the oven and set on a wire cooling rack. Leave to cool completely, then cut into 24 pieces. Store in an airtight container and eat within 4 days.

I'M OFTEN ASKED FOR A BROWNIE RECIPE WITHOUT FLOUR, AND THIS ONE IS QUITE WONDERFUL. IT IS INCREDIBLY RICH AND STICKY, AND IS BEST SERVED WITH A SCOOP OF ICE CREAM. AS WITH A LOT OF CHOCOLATE CAKES, IT IS AT ITS BEST MADE A DAY IN ADVANCE.

Flourless sticky brownies

300 g good dark chocolate, coarsely chopped

225 g unsalted butter, diced

3 large eggs, at room temperature

225 g light muscovado sugar

75 g ground almonds

1 teaspoon baking powder

100 g walnut pieces

a 25.5 x 20.5-cm baking tin, greased and base-lined with greaseproof paper

MAKES 24

Preheat the oven to 180°C (350°F) Gas 4.

Melt the chocolate and butter in a heatproof bowl set over a pan of steaming but not boiling water. Do not let the base of the bowl touch the water. Stir frequently until melted, then remove the bowl from the heat and leave to cool until needed.

Put the eggs and sugar into the bowl of an electric mixer and whisk until very pale, thick and mousse-like, about 3 minutes.

Using a large metal spoon, fold in the melted chocolate mixture. Combine the ground almonds with the baking powder and mix in, followed by the walnuts.

Transfer the mixture to the prepared tin and spread evenly. Bake in the preheated oven for about 40 minutes until just firm to touch and a cocktail stick or skewer inserted about halfway between the sides and the centre comes out clean.

Remove the tin from the oven and set on a wire rack. Leave to cool completely, then cut into 24 pieces, or if possible, wrap the entire brownie in foil or greaseproof paper and leave for a day before cutting. Store in an airtight container and eat within 5 days.

IF YOU WANT ALL THE FRAGRANCES AND FLAVOURS OF
A CHRISTMAS CAKE BUT DON'T WANT THE WORK, THIS
MELT-AND-MIX CAKE IS A GREAT ALTERNATIVE. IT'S GOT
DRIED FRUIT, SPICES AND ALCOHOL BUT IS LOW IN FAT,
MADE WITHOUT EGGS AND CAN BE SERVED WITH JUST
A DUSTING OF ICING SUGAR.

Cider fruit squares

50 g unsalted butter
200 g light muscovado sugar
100 g raisins
100 g sultanas
50 g ready-to-eat, dried
apricots, roughly chopped
175 ml dry cider
1 teaspoon mixed spice
1 teaspoon ground ginger
225 g fine plain
wholemeal flour
2 teaspoons baking powder
a good pinch of salt
icing sugar, to dust

*a 25.5 x 20.5-cm baking tin,
greased and base-lined with
greaseproof paper*

MAKES 24

In a saucepan large enough to hold all the ingredients, put the butter, sugar, raisins, sultanas, chopped apricots, cider, mixed spice, ground ginger and 175 ml water. Bring to the boil, stirring frequently, then reduce the heat and simmer gently for 2 minutes.

Remove the pan from the heat and leave to cool. Meanwhile, preheat the oven to 180°C (350°F) Gas 4.

Sift the flour, baking powder and salt into the pan, adding any fine pieces of bran left in the sieve. Mix with a wooden spoon until thoroughly combined.

Pour the mixture into the prepared tin and spread evenly. Bake in the preheated oven for about 25 minutes until a good golden brown and firm to the touch.

Remove from the oven and set on a wire rack to leave to cool completely. The cake tastes best if covered tightly and left overnight before cutting. Cut into 24 squares and dust with icing sugar. Store in an airtight container and eat within 1 week.

LEMON SQUARES AND BARS ARE EVER-POPULAR AND A
STAPLE OF MANY A BAKE SALE AND COFFEE MORNING.
BUT FOR CHRISTMAS I LIKE TO MAKE THIS RICHER FRENCH
VERSION, USING THICK CREAM RATHER THAN FLOUR IN
THE FILLING — AND IT'S JUST AS EASY TO MAKE.

Lemon squares

For the base

150 g plain flour

4 tablespoons icing sugar

**finely grated zest of
½ unwaxed lemon**

**115 g unsalted butter,
chilled and diced**

For the topping

**3 large eggs,
at room temperature**

**175 g icing sugar, sifted,
plus extra to dust**

**finely grated zest of
2 unwaxed lemons**

**freshly squeezed juice
of 4 lemons**

125 ml double cream

*a 20.5-cm square baking tin,
lined with aluminium foil*

MAKES 12

Preheat the oven to 180°C (350°F) Gas 4.

To make the base, put the flour, icing sugar and lemon zest into the bowl of a food processor and process for a few seconds until combined. Add the butter and process to make fine crumbs.

Tip into the prepared baking tin and press onto the base with your fingers to make an even layer. Bake in the preheated oven for about 25 minutes until firm and pale golden. Remove from the oven and leave to cool while you make the topping.

To make the topping, crack the eggs into a large jug and beat with a small whisk until broken up. Add the sugar and whisk until thoroughly combined. Add the lemon zest and juice and mix thoroughly, then work in the cream.

Return the tin to the oven and slightly pull out the shelf just enough so you can pour the filling into the tin. Gently push the shelf back into place, then close the door and reduce the temperature to 160°C (325°F) Gas 3. Bake for about 25 minutes until just firm.

Put the tin on a wire cooling rack and leave to cool completely, then cover lightly and chill overnight. Use the foil to lift the whole square out of the tin, then cut into 12 pieces. Dust with icing sugar and serve. Store in an airtight container in the fridge and eat within 3 days.

A RICH CHOCOLATE TREAT TO SERVE IN THIN SLICES WITH COFFEE OR
WHIPPED CREAM FOR DESSERT. THERE'S NO BAKING INVOLVED AS IT'S
MADE FROM MELTING VERY GOOD BITTER CHOCOLATE WITH BUTTER,
THEN MIXING WITH WHISKED EGGS AND SUGAR AND FLAVOURING WITH
BRANDY (OR WALNUT LIQUEUR IF YOU CAN FIND IT), TOASTED WALNUTS
AND THE BEST DRIED CRANBERRIES YOU CAN FIND (SEE PAGE 39).

Chocolate brandy cake

250 g dark chocolate,
coarsely chopped

250 g unsalted butter, diced

250 g digestive biscuits

2 large eggs,
at room temperature

4 tablespoons caster sugar

150 g walnut halves,
lightly toasted

100 g ready-to-eat,
soft-dried cranberries

4 tablespoons brandy or
walnut liqueur

cocoa powder, to dust

*a 22-cm springform tin,
lined with clingfilm*

MAKES 16 SLICES

Melt the chocolate and butter in a heatproof bowl set over a pan
of steaming but not boiling water. Do not let the base of the bowl
touch the water. Stir frequently until melted, then remove the bowl
from the heat and leave to cool until needed. Coarsely crush the
biscuits with a rolling pin or in a food processor.

Using an electric or rotary whisk, beat the eggs with the sugar until
very thick and mousse-like and the whisk leaves a ribbon-like trail
when lifted out of the bowl. Whisk in the melted chocolate mixture.

Coarsely chop 100 g of the walnuts and carefully fold in with the
cranberries, brandy and the crushed biscuits.

Spoon into the prepared tin and spread evenly. Decorate with the
rest of the walnut halves. Cover the top of the tin with clingfilm
and chill for at least 4 hours or overnight.

When ready to serve, unclip the tin and remove the clingfilm.
Dust with cocoa and serve cut into thin slices. Store in an airtight
container in the fridge for up to 1 week.

THE SWEDISH FESTIVAL OF ST LUCIA ON 13TH DECEMBER HAS A COMPLEX HISTORY. OVER TIME IT HAS ABSORBED A PAGAN WINTER SOLSTICE FESTIVAL, THE FEAST OF ST NICHOLAS AND A MODERN FESTIVAL OF LIGHT. THIS GOLDEN CAKE, MADE FOR THE FESTIVAL, USES SAFFRON FOR THE FLAVOUR AND THE SYMBOLISM OF THE COLOUR. SERVE WITH WHIPPED CREAM AND RED FRUIT CONSERVE (PAGE 92).

Swedish saffron cake

125 ml milk
225 g slightly salted butter
1 teaspoon saffron threads
2 large eggs,
at room temperature
200 g golden caster sugar
225 g plain flour
2 teaspoons baking powder
icing sugar, to dust

*a 22–23-cm springform tin,
greased, base-lined with greaseproof
paper and sprinkled with dried
breadcrumbs or ground almonds*

MAKES ONE MEDIUM CAKE

Heat the milk with the butter until melted and steaming hot but not boiling. Remove the pan from the heat and sprinkle in the saffron. Cover the pan and leave to infuse for 1 hour.

When ready, preheat the oven to 180°C (350°F) Gas 4.

Put the eggs into the bowl of an electric mixer and whisk until just frothy. Whisk in the sugar and continue whisking until very thick and mousse-like and the whisk leaves a ribbon-like trail when lifted out of the bowl.

Gently fold in the just-warm saffron mixture. Sift the flour and baking powder into the bowl and fold in gently with a large metal spoon – the mixture will look hopeless at first but it will combine after a minute.

Pour into the prepared tin and bake in the preheated oven for 35–40 minutes until the cake is a good golden brown, slightly shrunk from the sides of the tin and firm to touch.

Put on a wire rack and unclip the tin. Leave to cool completely then serve dusted with icing sugar. Store in an airtight container and eat within 4 days. Not suitable for freezing.

THIS FESTIVE CAKE, BASED ON A FRENCH QUATRE-QUARTS OR POUND
CAKE, IS A RICH LEMON SPONGE STUDDED WITH PECANS AND DRIED
CRANBERRIES (SEE PAGE 39). FOR A SPECIAL TOUCH, DECORATE WITH
FRESH CRANBERRIES DIPPED IN BEATEN EGG WHITE, ROLLED IN CASTER
SUGAR AND LEFT TO DRY FOR 24 HOURS ON NON-STICK BAKING PAPER.

Lemon pecan cake

200 g pecan halves

200 g ready-to-eat,
soft-dried cranberries

200 g plain flour

225 g unsalted butter,
at room temperature

200 g caster sugar

finely grated zest and juice of
1 unwaxed lemon

4 large eggs, at room
temperature, separated

a good pinch of salt

1 teaspoon baking powder

icing sugar, to dust

frosted cranberries (optional),
see introduction above

ribbon, to decorate

*a 22-cm springform tin,
greased and lined with
greaseproof paper*

MAKES ONE MEDIUM CAKE

Preheat the oven to 150°C (300°F) Gas 2.

Put the pecans and cranberries in a bowl with a couple of tablespoons of the
flour and toss well to break up any clumps of fruit. Set aside until needed.

Beat the butter until very soft and creamy using an electric mixer or
wooden spoon. Add the sugar and lemon zest and beat well until fluffy.
Beat in the egg yolks, one at a time, then beat in the lemon juice.

Sift the remaining flour, the salt and baking powder into the bowl and
gently fold in using a large metal spoon. Add the pecan-cranberry mixture
and fold in.

Whisk the egg whites in a spotless, grease-free bowl until stiff peaks form,
then fold into the cake mixture in 3 batches.

Spoon into the prepared tin and spread evenly. Bake in the preheated oven
for about 1¼ hours or until lightly golden and a cocktail stick inserted into
the centre of the cake comes out clean (if there is damp batter on the stick
return the cake to the oven and bake for about 5 minutes longer and test
again). Set the tin on a wire rack and leave to cool completely. Remove the
cake from the tin and discard the greaseproof paper. Wrap in fresh paper
and store in an airtight container for at least 24 hours before cutting. Serve
dusted with icing sugar (you can use a stencil in the shape of a star or tree)
and tied with a ribbon. Decorate with frosted cranberries if desired (see
introduction above). Eat within 2 weeks or freeze for up to 1 month.

IF YOU WANT WARM BRIOCHES ON THE TABLE FOR BREAKFAST, YOU CAN
MAKE AND SHAPE THE DOUGH THE NIGHT BEFORE, READY FOR BAKING IN
THE MORNING. NORMALLY THE DOUGH GETS THREE RISINGS BUT MY SON
CAME UP WITH THIS SIMPLER AND MUCH QUICKER VARIATION.

Chocolate brioches

500 g unbleached strong
white bread flour

a 7-g sachet easy-blend
dried yeast

1 teaspoon salt

175 g unsalted butter, diced

50 g caster sugar

3 large eggs,
at room temperature

150 ml milk, lukewarm

100 g dark chocolate,
coarsely chopped

beaten egg, to glaze

*a 12-hole muffin tray, silicone
or well-greased non-stick metal*

MAKES 12

Put the flour, yeast and salt in the bowl of a large electric mixer and mix
by hand. Add the butter and rub into the flour with your fingertips until the
mixture looks like fine crumbs. Mix in the sugar. Beat the eggs with the milk
until thoroughly combined, then add to the flour mixture. Using the dough
hook attachment of the mixer, mix the ingredients on low speed until you
get a heavy, sticky dough. Scrape down the sides, then knead the dough in
the machine on low speed for 5 minutes until glossy, very smooth and soft.
If you don't have a food mixer, mix the ingredients as above, then knead
the dough by hand. Cover and leave to rise at normal room temperature
(not too warm) until doubled in size, 1½–2 hours.

Turn out the risen dough onto a lightly floured work surface. Punch down,
then work in the chopped chocolate, kneading gently for about 1 minute.
Divide the dough into 12 equal portions. Pinch off a hazelnut-sized ball from
each portion and roll into a smooth, neat ball. Shape the rest of the portion
into a neat ball and drop into the muffin tray. Flour your index finger and
push into the centre of the dough in the tray, then place the smaller ball
over this hole. Repeat with the remaining portions of dough. Slip the tray
into a large plastic bag, slightly inflate, then leave to rise until doubled in
size, about 1 hour in a warm kitchen or overnight in the fridge.

When ready to continue, preheat the oven to 200°C (400°F) Gas 6.

Uncover the brioches and lightly brush with beaten egg to glaze. Bake in
the preheated oven for 18–20 minutes until firm and a good golden colour.
Leave to cool for a minute for the crust to firm up then carefully turn out
onto a wire rack. Eat warm or leave to cool completely, then store in an
airtight container and eat within 24 hours or freeze for up to 1 month.

NOT AS SWEET AS SOME MUFFINS, THESE ARE GOOD FOR BRUNCH AND BREAKFAST ALONG WITH SOME GOOD COFFEE DURING THE FESTIVE WEEKEND WHEN FRESH OR FROZEN CRANBERRIES ARE AROUND.

Christmas mini-muffins

150 g plain flour

1 teaspoon baking powder

a pinch of salt

50 g caster sugar

finely grated zest of ½ unwaxed orange

50 g pecan pieces, coarsely chopped, plus 2 tablespoons, to decorate

1½ tablespoons raisins

50 g fresh or frozen cranberries (no need to thaw)

1 large egg, beaten

50 g unsalted butter, melted

75 ml milk

icing sugar, to dust

mini-muffin trays lined with foil mini-muffin cases, or use double cases set on a baking tray

MAKES 30

Preheat the oven to 180°C (350°F) Gas 4.

Sift the flour, baking powder and salt into a mixing bowl. Stir in the sugar, orange zest, chopped pecans and raisins.

Put the cranberries into the bowl of a food processor and chop roughly. Stir into the flour mixture.

Combine the beaten egg with the melted butter and milk and stir into the flour mixture with a wooden spoon.

Spoon the mixture into the foil cases using 2 teaspoons, then decorate with the extra pecans. Bake in the preheated oven for 12–15 minutes until barely golden and firm to the touch.

Turn out onto a wire rack. Serve warm, dusted with icing sugar. When cold, store in an airtight container and eat within 2 days.

FOR PARTIES, BRUNCHES AND OFFICE TREATS, SMALL,
ONE-BITE MUFFINS ARE ALWAYS POPULAR AND EASILY
TRANSPORTED. THESE CAN BE LEFT PLAIN, DUSTED
WITH ICING SUGAR OR DECORATED WITH PIPED ICING
(SEE PAGES 15 AND 16), EXTRA NUTS OR CHOC CHIPS.
USE CONTRASTING CHOC CHIPS FOR THE BEST EFFECT.

Double choc mini–muffins

50 g unsalted butter,
at room temperature

50 g caster sugar

1 large egg, beaten

125 ml soured cream

50 g white, dark or milk choc
chips, plus extra to decorate

125 g plain flour

25 g unsweetened cocoa powder

½ teaspoon baking powder

½ teaspoon bicarbonate of soda

a pinch of salt

icing sugar, to dust

*mini-muffin trays lined with foil
mini-muffin cases, or use double
cases set on a baking tray*

MAKES ABOUT 30

Preheat the oven to 180°C (350°F) Gas 4.

Put the butter and sugar in a mixing bowl and beat with a
wooden spoon until fluffy. Beat in the egg until thoroughly
combined. Finally, beat in the soured cream followed by the
chocolate chips.

Sift the flour, cocoa, baking powder, bicarbonate of soda and
salt into the bowl and combine without over-mixing.

Spoon the mixture into the foil cases using 2 teaspoons, then
decorate with a few extra choc chips. Bake in the preheated
oven for 12–15 minutes until firm to the touch.

Leave to cool on a wire rack and serve dusted with icing sugar.
Store in an airtight container and eat within 2 days.

SPICY, STICKY AND UTTERLY MOREISH. PARTICULARLY POPULAR WITH CHILDREN, YOU CAN GET THEM TO DECORATE THE MUFFINS WITH WRITING ICING PENS AND GIVE THEM AS GIFTS TO THEIR FRIENDS.

Gingerbread mini-muffins

100 g unsalted butter
2 tablespoons black treacle
2 tablespoons honey
100 g dark muscovado sugar
100 ml milk
175 g plain flour
1 teaspoon bicarbonate of soda
1 tablespoon ground ginger
1 teaspoon ground cinnamon
a good pinch of salt
1 large egg, beaten
50 g stem ginger, drained and finely chopped

To decorate
royal or glacé icing, or writing icing pens

mini-muffin trays lined with foil mini-muffin cases, or use double cases set on a baking tray

MAKES ABOUT 36

Preheat the oven to 180°C (350°F) Gas 4.

Put the butter, treacle, honey, sugar and milk in a saucepan over low heat and melt gently. Remove from the heat and leave to cool for a couple of minutes.

Meanwhile, sift the flour, bicarbonate of soda, ground ginger, cinnamon and salt into a mixing bowl. Pour in the cooled, melted mixture, then the egg. Mix thoroughly with a wooden spoon. Mix in the stem ginger.

Spoon the mixture into the cases using 2 teaspoons. Bake in the preheated oven for 15 minutes until firm to the touch.

Leave to cool on a wire rack, then decorate with icing. Store in an airtight container and eat within 3 days.

A QUICK AND EASY RECIPE WITH A RICH FLAVOUR.
AND SINCE ALMOST EVERYONE LOVES FUDGE, AN
OFFERING OF A FEW SQUARES OF THIS WILL PUT
A SMILE ON ANYONE'S FACE.

Chocolate and cream fudge

100 g dark chocolate,
coarsely chopped

55 g unsalted butter, diced

2 tablespoons single or
whipping cream

1 teaspoon vanilla extract
or dark rum

1 tablespoon golden syrup

225 g icing sugar, sifted

a shallow, 18-cm square tin,
greased

MAKES 20 SQUARES

Melt the chocolate and butter in a heatproof bowl set over a pan of steaming but not boiling water. Do not let the base of the bowl touch the water. Stir frequently until melted, then remove the bowl from the heat and gently stir in the cream, then the vanilla extract, followed by the golden syrup.

Using a wooden spoon, then your hands, work in the icing sugar 1 tablespoon at a time, to make a thick, smooth fudge. If the mixture starts to stiffen before all the sugar has been incorporated, return the bowl to the heat for a minute or so.

Transfer the mixture to the prepared tin and press in evenly. Chill until firm, then turn out and cut into squares with a large, sharp knife. Keep in the fridge and eat within 10 days.

THIS RECIPE IS GREAT FOR CHRISTMAS AS THE ROUND TRUFFLES CAN BE LEFT PLAIN OR DECORATED WITH SCRAPS OF RED AND GREEN COLOURED SUGAR PASTE (OR READY-ROLL ICING) TO LOOK LIKE HOLLY BERRIES AND LEAVES, OR WITH ROYAL ICING (SEE PAGE 15) TO RESEMBLE A TRADITIONAL 'CANNON BALL' CHRISTMAS PUDDING. YOU CAN ALSO ADD A SPLASH OF BRANDY OR RUM TO THE MIXTURE.

Christmas truffles

200 g dark chocolate, coarsely chopped

125 g chocolate spongecake crumbs

60 g ground almonds

cocoa powder, to dust

foil petits-fours or mini-muffin cases

Melt the chocolate in a heatproof bowl set over a pan of steaming but not boiling water. Do not let the base of the bowl touch the water. Stir occasionally until melted, then remove the bowl from the heat.

Stir in the spongecake crumbs and ground almonds. When thoroughly combined, cover the bowl and chill until firm, about 30 minutes. The mixture can be kept in the fridge, tightly covered, for up to 3 days.

Using a teaspoon of mixture for each truffle, roll the mixture into neat balls with your hands then drop into a small bowl of cocoa and shake to lightly coat. Set each truffle in a foil case. Chill until firm, then pack into boxes or store in an airtight container. Keep in a cool place or the fridge and and eat within 1 week.

Savoury treats

IT'S HARD TO EAT JUST ONE OF THESE CRISP, SAVOURY CRACKERS, SO THEY'RE PERFECT WITH DRINKS AT PARTY TIME, OR WITH A BOWL OF SOUP. THE RECIPE COMES FROM ALYSON COOK, WHO CATERS TO THE STARS OF HOLLYWOOD.

Parmesan herb crisps

85 g Parmesan or Grana Padano cheese, grated

130 g plain flour

110 g unsalted butter, chilled and diced

½ teaspoon dried *herbes de Provence*

½ teaspoon Worcestershire sauce

2 tablespoons white wine (optional)

non-stick baking paper

several baking trays, greased

MAKES 50–60

Put all the ingredients in a food processor and blend until the mixture forms a ball of dough.

Remove the dough from the processor and put on a sheet of non-stick baking paper. Shape into a log about 30 x 2.5 cm. Wrap tightly in clingfilm, then chill until firm, about 2 hours. The mixture can be kept in the fridge, tightly wrapped, for up to 4 days.

When ready to cook, preheat the oven to 190°C (375°F) Gas 5.

Cut the log into 5-mm slices. Arrange the slices well apart on the prepared baking trays and bake in the preheated oven for 12–15 minutes until light golden.

Leave to cool on the trays for 2 minutes, then transfer the crisps to a wire rack to cool completely. Store in an airtight container and eat within 5 days or freeze for up to 1 month.

THESE ATTRACTIVE SAVOURY BISCUITS FROM FRANCE ARE MADE FROM PUFF PASTRY FOLDED UP WITH A MIXTURE OF CHEESE AND MUSTARD, AND ARE QUITE SIMPLE TO ASSEMBLE. CHOOSE THE ALL-BUTTER KIND OF READY-MADE PASTRY FOR THE BEST FLAVOUR AND FLAKINESS.

Cheese palmiers

100 g Parmesan or Grana Padano cheese, finely grated

375 g all-butter puff pastry, thawed if necessary

1 tablespoon Dijon mustard

½ teaspoon mild paprika

¼ teaspoon cayenne pepper or ground black pepper

several baking trays, lined with non-stick baking paper

MAKES 36

Sprinkle a little of the grated cheese on the work surface and gently unroll the pastry, or if necessary, roll out to a rectangle about 23 x 38 cm. Spread the mustard over the pastry with a round-bladed knife. Mix the rest of the cheese with the paprika and pepper, then scatter over the pastry.

Now fold the pastry – it is supposed to resemble a palm leaf – but don't fold too tightly or the pastry won't puff up in the oven. Fold each long side over towards the centre, then fold each side over again so there are 4 layers of pastry on each side of the centre. Then fold one folded side of pastry on top of the other to make a log shape. Using a sharp knife, cut into slices about 1 cm thick. Arrange the slices on the prepared baking trays spaced well apart to allow for spreading, and leave the 2 halves of the 'U' shape slightly open so the pastry can puff up.

Chill for 15 minutes. Meanwhile, preheat the oven to 220°C (425°F) Gas 7.

Bake in the preheated oven for 8–10 minutes until crisp, well-puffed and golden. Transfer to a wire rack and leave to cool. Store in an airtight container and eat within 1 day – if necessary warm in a low oven before serving to crisp up.

Sweet, sticky palmiers – Sprinkle the work surface with caster sugar and unroll or roll out the pastry as above. Sprinkle with 3 tablespoons sugar mixed with 1 teaspoon ground cinnamon, then scatter over 2 tablespoons very finely chopped pecans. Press the nuts lightly into the pastry. Fold the dough as above and cut into slices, chill and bake – they will brown quicker than the cheese palmiers so watch them carefully.

RICHLY FLAVOURED WITH GOOD GRUYÈRE CHEESE AND
SPIKED WITH CHILLI, THESE SMALL CRISP PUFFS ARE
DELICIOUS WITH A GLASS OF WINE OR BOWL OF SOUP.
THEY CAN BE BAKED A DAY OR SO IN ADVANCE, THEN
GENTLY WARMED BEFORE SERVING.

Chilli cheese gougères

75 g unsalted butter, diced

¼ teaspoon salt

**¼–½ teaspoon dried red
chilli flakes, to taste**

100 g plain flour

3 large eggs, beaten

**125 g Gruyère cheese, finely
diced, plus 25 g finely grated**

*several baking trays,
greased and sprinkled with water*

MAKES 40

Put the butter, salt, chilli flakes and 185 ml water into a medium
pan. Heat gently until the butter has melted, then quickly bring
to the boil. Remove the pan from the heat and tip in the flour.
Beat well with a wooden spoon – don't worry that the mixture
looks a mess to begin with as it will come together to make a
smooth, shiny dough with a minute or so of vigorous beating.
Return the pan to the heat and stir over low heat for 1 minute.
Tip the dough into the bowl of an electric mixer and leave to
cool completely.

When nearly cool, preheat the oven to 220°C (425°F) Gas 7.

Gradually beat the eggs into the cooled dough in the mixer,
beating well after each addition. Stir in the diced Gruyère.

Using 2 teaspoons, spoon the mixture into small heaps of about
a teaspoonful on the prepared baking trays, spacing them well
apart. Sprinkle with the finely grated Gruyère, then bake in the
preheated oven for 10–15 minutes until golden brown and crisp.

Transfer the gougères to a wire rack and leave to cool. Store in
an airtight container and eat within 3 days. Warm gently in the
oven before serving.

CRISP, BUTTERY SAVOURY CHEESE BISCUITS SIMPLY
MADE IN A FOOD PROCESSOR. SMOKED PAPRIKA ADDS
AN INTRIGUING TASTE ALTHOUGH YOU COULD USE A
LITTLE COARSELY GROUND BLACK PEPPER OR A VERY
LITTLE RED-HOT CAYENNE PEPPER INSTEAD.

Walnut sablés

100 g plain flour

100 g unsalted butter,
chilled and diced

½ teaspoon smoked mild paprika

100 g Parmesan or Grana
Padano cheese, finely grated

100 g walnut pieces

1 large egg yolk

1–2 baking trays, lightly greased

MAKES 20

Put the flour, butter, paprika and cheese into the bowl of a food
processor. Run the machine until the mixture looks like fine
crumbs. Add the nuts and the egg yolk and run the machine
until the dough comes together into a ball.

Turn the dough out of the bowl, flour your hands and shape into
a brick about 13 x 6 x 4.5 cm. Wrap in clingfilm and chill until
firm, about 30 minutes. The mixture can be kept in the fridge,
tightly wrapped, for up to 3 days.

When ready to continue, preheat the oven to 190°C (375°F)
Gas 5.

Using a large, sharp knife, cut the brick of dough into 20 even
slices. Arrange slightly apart on the prepared baking trays, then
bake in the preheated oven for 12–15 minutes until golden
brown and just firm.

Remove the trays from the oven and set on a wire rack. Leave to
cool completely before lifting off the sablés. Store in an airtight
container and eat within 3 days.

HOME-MADE BREADSTICKS LOOK AND TASTE SO MUCH BETTER THAN THE TYPE FROM THE SUPERMARKET. SERVE IN TALL GLASS JUGS FOR PARTIES ALONGSIDE DIPS, SPREADS AND SOFT CHEESES. THE BASIC DOUGH IS DIVIDED INTO 3 AND INDIVIDUALLY FLAVOURED.

Grissini

500 g unbleached strong white bread flour

a 7-g sachet easy-blend dried yeast

2 teaspoons sea salt

275 ml tepid water

4 tablespoons olive oil

25 g Parmesan or Grana Padano cheese, grated

2 tablespoons sesame seeds

25 g stoned black olives, chopped

several baking trays, lightly greased

MAKES 36

Combine the flour, yeast and salt in a large mixing bowl or the bowl of a large electric mixer. Make a well in the centre and pour in the water and oil. Gradually work the ingredients together – use the dough hook attachment of the mixer on low speed – to make a fairly firm dough. If necessary, add a little more water or flour.

Turn out the dough onto a lightly floured work surface and knead for 10 minutes until very elastic or 5 minutes using the mixer.

Divide the dough into 3 portions. Add half the Parmesan to one portion and work in. Add half the sesame seeds to the second portion and work in. Finally, work all the chopped olives into the last portion.

Place each portion in a different bowl, cover and leave in a warm place until doubled in size, about 1 hour.

When ready to continue, preheat the oven to 230°C (450°F) Gas 8.

Punch down each portion of dough, then knead for 30 seconds on a lightly floured work surface. Divide each portion of dough into 12 equal pieces. Using your hands, roll each to a thin sausage about 30 cm long. Arrange slightly apart on the prepared baking trays. Lightly brush the grissini with water then sprinkle the remaining cheese over the cheese grissini and the remaining sesame seeds over the sesame ones. Leave the olive grissini plain. Bake in the preheated oven for about 15 minutes until crisp and golden.

Transfer to a wire rack and leave to cool. Store in an airtight container and eat within 4 days. Gently warm in the oven before serving to crisp up.

Spicy nuts

THE GREAT THING ABOUT MAKING SPICY NUTS IS THAT THEY ARE ABSOLUTELY FRESH AND CRUNCHY AND YOU KNOW WHAT'S IN THE MIX. LOOK OUT FOR LARGE BAGS OF MIXED NUTS – CASHEWS, BRAZILS, ALMONDS, PECANS, HAZELNUTS AND WALNUTS. ANY LEFTOVER NUTS CAN BE STIRRED INTO A PILAFF OR COUSCOUS.

2 tablespoons olive oil
350 g unsalted mixed nuts
1 tablespoon light muscovado sugar
1 tablespoon Japanese soy sauce
¼–½ teaspoon cayenne pepper
¼–½ teaspoon ground black pepper
½ teaspoon smoked mild paprika

SERVES ABOUT 8

Heat the oil in a non-stick frying pan. Add the nuts, stir well, then add all the other ingredients and stir-fry over medium heat for about 5 minutes until golden.

Tip into a heatproof bowl and leave to cool.

Serve the same day or store in an airtight container and eat within 2 days.

Marinated olives

OLIVES IN A DELICIOUS MARINADE CAN BE PART OF AN ANTIPASTI SPREAD, HANDED ROUND WITH DRINKS OR ADDED TO PIZZAS AND SALADS. THE FLAVOURED OIL CAN BE RECYCLED FOR DRESSINGS AND MARINADES.

250 g black olives (Kalamata or Niçoise)
2 garlic cloves, thinly sliced
2 fresh rosemary sprigs
2 fresh thyme sprigs
2 fresh oregano sprigs
pared rind of 1 unwaxed lemon, in strips
good extra virgin olive oil, to cover

a sterilized glass jar and lid (see page 4)

SERVES ABOUT 8

Rinse the olives and drain well.

Put the garlic, sprigs of herbs and strips of lemon rind into the sterilized jar with about 4 tablespoons of the olive oil. Close the jar and shake well. Open up the jar and add the olives, then close the jar and gently shake it again so the olives are well coated in the marinade. Open the jar and fill with enough oil to well cover the olives. Seal and shake gently, then keep in the fridge for 2 weeks to marinate before using. Once opened, keep in the fridge, immersed in oil, and eat within 7–10 days. Serve at room temperature.

Preserves

I ALWAYS MAKE A BATCH OF THIS JEWEL-BRIGHT RUBY
RELISH TO GO WITH OUR THANKSGIVING TURKEY — I
LOVE THE RICH, FRUITY AROMA THAT FILLS THE HOUSE
WHEN IT'S COOKING. IT GOES INTO THE SANDWICHES
WITH COLD TURKEY AND HAM, OR SIMPLY ALONGSIDE
SOME MATURE CHEDDAR. I TRY TO KEEP SOME FOR
CHRISTMAS BUT IT'S USUALLY ALL GONE BY THEN!

Cranberry and basil relish

2 tablespoons olive oil

1 medium red onion,
finely chopped

2 garlic cloves, crushed

350 g fresh or frozen
cranberries (no need to thaw)

100 g demerara sugar

50 ml red wine vinegar

a small bunch of fresh basil,
leaves only

¼ teaspoon sea salt

several grinds of black pepper

several sterilized glass jars and lids
(see page 4)

MAKES 400 ML

Heat the olive oil in a large, heavy frying pan or sauté pan,
preferably non-stick. Add the onion and garlic and cook gently,
stirring occasionally, for 5 minutes.

Add the rest of the ingredients to the pan and stir well. Cook over
medium heat, stirring frequently, until very thick, about 10 minutes.
Taste and adjust the seasoning, adding more salt or pepper as
needed. Spoon into the sterilized jars and seal. When completely
cold, keep in the fridge and use within 1 month.

A BRIGHT AND ZINGY RELISH THAT CAN BE MADE AT ANY TIME OF THE YEAR, HOWEVER IT IS PARTICULARLY GOOD WITH COLD HAM AND CHEESE, SO IT MAKES AN EXCELLENT PRESENT DURING THE FESTIVE SEASON.

Ginger fruit relish

5 medium or large
unwaxed oranges

2 pears

2 apples, fairly tart

6 tablespoons white
wine vinegar

200 g light muscovado sugar

5 cm fresh ginger,
peeled and grated

1 teaspoon sea salt

40 g raisins

grated zest and freshly squeezed
juice of 1 unwaxed lemon

*several sterilized glass jars and lids
(see page 4)*

MAKES ABOUT 800 ML

Rinse the oranges, then grate the zest and reserve. Using a serrated knife, peel the oranges to remove all the skin and the white pith. Cut into small chunks, discarding the pips.

Peel and core the pears and apples, and cut into chunks the same size as the oranges.

Put the vinegar and sugar into a large, heavy, non-aluminium pan and heat gently, stirring frequently to dissolve the sugar.

Add the grated ginger and salt to the pan. Bring to the boil, then stir in the chopped fruit. Boil gently for 20 minutes, stirring frequently until the fruit is very soft.

Stir in the reserved orange zest, the raisins and the grated lemon zest and juice.

Cook for another 10–15 minutes, stirring frequently, until very thick and no longer watery on top.

Remove the pan from the heat and stir well. Spoon into the sterilized jars and seal. Leave to cool, then store in a cool spot for up to 1 month. Once opened, keep in the fridge.

A SLIGHTLY SPICY, SWEET GOLDEN SPREAD FOR
BREAKFAST MUFFINS, BRIOCHE, TOAST OR WARM
BREAD ROLLS. IF YOU LIKE THE WARM, LEMONY
FLAVOUR OF PRESERVED GINGER, ADD 25 G STEM
GINGER, DRAINED AND FINELY CHOPPED, RIGHT
AT THE END OF THE COOKING TIME.

Maple squash butter

1 kg butternut squash

100 ml pure apple juice

½–1 teaspoon ground ginger, to taste

100 ml maple syrup

a cinnamon stick

several sterilized glass jars and lids (see page 4)

MAKES 600 ML

Preheat the oven to 180°C (350°F) Gas 4.

Halve the squash then scoop out the seeds. Set the two halves skin-side down in a baking dish. Cover tightly with foil then bake in the preheated oven until tender, about 1¼–1½ hours.

Remove the squash from the oven and leave until cool enough to handle. Peel off the skin and dice the flesh. Put the flesh into the bowl of a food processor with the apple juice, ground ginger and maple syrup and process until smooth.

Tip the purée into a heavy pan, add the cinnamon stick and set over medium heat. Bring to the boil, then cook until very thick, about 10 minutes, stirring very frequently to prevent the mixture from catching.

Spoon into the sterilized jars and seal. Leave to cool, then keep in the fridge and use within 2 weeks.

FROZEN RED FRUITS ARE AVAILABLE ALL YEAR ROUND AND ALWAYS MAKE A USEFUL ADDITION TO THE FREEZER. THIS RECIPE, MADE WITH A LARGE BAG CONTAINING RASPBERRIES, STRAWBERRIES, CHERRIES, BLUEBERRIES, REDCURRANTS AND BLACKCURRANTS, MAKES A JUICY, THICK CONSERVE TO SERVE WARM OR AT ROOM TEMPERATURE WITH PANCAKES AND WAFFLES, ICE CREAM, MUFFINS, BRIOCHE OR SPONGE PUDDINGS.

Red fruit conserve

1 kg frozen unsweetened red fruits

200 g caster sugar

1 tablespoon lemon juice

a 340-g jar redcurrant jelly

several sterilized glass jars and lids (see page 4)

MAKES 1.2 L

Put the frozen fruits, sugar, lemon juice and redcurrant jelly into a large non-metallic bowl. Cover and leave for 2–4 hours, or overnight in the fridge, until the fruit has thawed.

Tip the mixture into a large, heavy, non-aluminium pan and bring to the boil. Simmer steadily until the mixture has thickened, about 10 minutes. Remove the pan from the heat, stir gently, then spoon into the sterilized jars and seal. Leave to cool, then keep in the fridge for up to 2 weeks.

Suppliers

Cake Craft Shop
www.cakecraftshop.co.uk
Tel: 01732 46 48 26
*This mail-order website stocks an
extensive range of plain and decorated
gift boxes for cakes, muffins, biscuits
etc. There are also boxes especially
for presenting chocolates, foil squares
to wrap around truffles, patterned
cellophane bags, piping sets, muffin
cases, ribbon and raffia.*

Cakes Cookies & Crafts Shop
www.cakescookiesandcraftsshop.co.uk
Tel: 01524 389 684
*Online suppliers of every kind of
baking equipment you might need:
cupcake cases, tins, silicone moulds,
biscuit cutters, edible decorations
and plenty more.*

Crafty Ribbons
www.craftyribbons.com
Every kind of ribbon imaginable.

Jane Asher
www.janeasher.com
22–24 Cale Street
London SW3 3QU
Tel: 020 7584 6177
*Britain's foremost cake and sugarcraft
supplier, for all your decoration needs!*

John Lewis
www.johnlewis.com
*A good range of bakeware including
biscuit cutters, as well as decorated
tins, boxes, papers and ribbons.*

Kitchenware
www.kitchenware.co.uk
Tel: 0870 8500520
*All sorts of kitchen and baking
equipment including baking tins, pretty
cake storage tins, piping and icing kits
and lots more.*

Lakeland
www.lakeland.co.uk
*A huge selection of kitchen and baking
equipment, such as cake decorations,
storage containers, preserving and
baking equipment, craft items, cake
tins, boxes of all sizes, biscuit cutters,
paper cases and decorations.*

Paperchase
www.paperchase.co.uk
*Stationery galore, including gorgeous
gift boxes, labels, wrapping paper
and more.*

Squires Shop
www.squires-shop.com
Tel: 0845 2255671
*Online specialist suppliers of all things
to do with cakes, including decorating,
food colouring and sugarcraft.*

V V Rouleaux
www.vvrouleaux.com
54 Sloane Square
Cliveden Place
London SW1W 8AX
Tel: 020 7730 3125
102 Marylebone Lane
London W1U 2QD
Tel: 020 7224 5179
*Purveyors of the finest ribbons
and decorations.*

Wares of Knutsford
www.waresofknutsford.co.uk
Tel: 08456 121273
*'Household and hardware emporium'
which prides itself on being a good old-
fashioned quality ironmongers selling
a selection of kitchen and bakeware
including shaped cake tins and biscuit
cutters, lots of jam-related tools
(such as jam jars, kilner jars, labels,
thermometers and funnels), paper
doilies and baking tins in every
imaginable shape and size.*

Index

A

almonds:
almond biscotti, 39
Christmas truffles, 68
Czech almond crescents, 35
flourless sticky brownies, 47
lebkuchen, 19
Sardinian almond biscuits,
28
apple juice:
maple squash butter, 91
apples:
ginger fruit relish, 88
apricots:
cider fruit squares, 48

B

basil:
cranberry and basil relish, 87
baskets, brandy snap, 32
biscotti:
almond biscotti, 39
chocolate chip biscotti, 40
biscuits:
cheese palmiers, 75
Czech almond crescents, 35
Dutch vanilla butter
biscuits, 23
French chocolate fingers, 31
gingerbread shapes, 15
iced honey and cinnamon
biscuits, 12
iced star biscuits, 16
lacy brandy snaps, 32
lebkuchen, 19
Parmesan herb crisps, 72
peanut butter choc
chunkies, 24
pistachio sablés, 36

Sardinian almond biscuits,
28
Swedish pepper biscuits, 20
triple chocolate cookies, 27
walnut sablés, 79
brandy:
brandy snap baskets, 32
chocolate brandy cake, 52
lacy brandy snaps, 32
breadsticks, 80
brioches, chocolate, 59
brownies:
flourless sticky brownies, 47
triple chocolate brownies, 44
butternut squash:
maple squash butter, 91

C

cakes:
chocolate brandy cake, 52
cider fruit squares, 48
flourless sticky brownies, 47
lemon pecan cake, 56
Swedish saffron cake, 55
triple chocolate brownies, 44
cheese:
cheese palmiers, 75
chilli cheese gougères, 76
grissini, 80
Parmesan herb crisps, 72
walnut sablés, 79
chilli cheese gougères, 76
chocolate:
chocolate and cream fudge,
67
chocolate brandy cake, 52
chocolate brioches, 59
chocolate chip biscotti, 40
Christmas truffles, 68

double choc mini-muffins, 63
flourless sticky brownies, 47
French chocolate fingers, 31
lacy brandy snaps, 32
lebkuchen, 19
peanut butter choc
chunkies, 24
triple chocolate brownies, 44
triple chocolate cookies, 27
Christmas mini-muffins, 60
Christmas tree decorations:
gingerbread shapes, 15
iced honey and cinnamon
biscuits, 12
iced star biscuits, 16
Christmas truffles, 68
cider fruit squares, 48
cinnamon:
gingerbread shapes, 15
gingerbread mini-muffins, 64
iced honey and cinnamon
biscuits, 12
lebkuchen, 19
maple squash butter, 91
conserve, red fruit, 92
cookies, triple chocolate, 27
cranberries (dried):
almond biscotti, 39
chocolate brandy cake, 52
Christmas mini-muffins, 60
lemon pecan cake, 56
cranberries (fresh):
cranberry and basil relish, 87
Czech almond crescents, 35

D

dried fruit:
almond biscotti, 39
chocolate brandy cake, 52

Christmas mini-muffins, 60
cider fruit squares, 48
lemon pecan cake, 56
Dutch vanilla butter biscuits,
23

F

flourless sticky brownies, 47
French chocolate fingers, 31
fruit:
ginger fruit relish, 88
red fruit conserve, 92
fudge, chocolate and cream, 67

G

ginger:
ginger fruit relish, 88
gingerbread mini-muffins, 64
gingerbread shapes, 15
lacy brandy snaps, 32
lebkuchen, 19
maple squash butter, 91
Swedish pepper biscuits, 20
glacé icing, 16
gougères, chilli cheese, 76
grissini, 80
Gruyère cheese:
chilli cheese gougères, 76

H

honey:
gingerbread mini-muffins, 64
iced honey and cinnamon
biscuits, 12

I

iced honey and cinnamon
biscuits, 12
iced star biscuits, 16

icing:
  glacé icing, 16
  royal icing, 15

L
lacy brandy snaps, 32
lebkuchen, 19
lemons:
  iced star biscuits, 16
  lemon pecan cake, 56
  lemon squares, 51
  marinated olives, 83

M
maple squash butter, 91
marinated olives, 83
muffins:
  Christmas mini-muffins, 60
  double choc mini-muffins, 63
  gingerbread mini-muffins, 64

N
nuts:
  almond biscotti, 39
  chocolate brandy cake, 52
  chocolate chip biscotti, 40
  Christmas mini-muffins, 60
  Christmas truffles, 68
  Czech almond crescents, 35
  flourless sticky brownies, 47
  lebkuchen, 19
  lemon pecan cake, 56
  peanut butter choc
    chunkies, 24
  pistachio sablés, 36
  Sardinian almond biscuits,
    28
  spicy nuts, 83
  triple chocolate cookies,
    27
  walnut sablés, 79

O
olives:
  grissini, 80
  marinated olives, 83
oranges:
  chocolate chip biscotti, 40
  Christmas mini-muffins, 60
  ginger fruit relish, 88
  Swedish pepper biscuits, 20
oregano:
  marinated olives, 83

P
palmiers, cheese, 75
Parmesan:
  cheese palmiers, 75
  grissini, 80
  Parmesan herb crisps, 72
  walnut sablés, 79
peanut butter choc chunkies,
  24
pears:
  ginger fruit relish, 88
pecan nuts:
  chocolate chip biscotti, 40
  Christmas mini-muffins, 60
  lemon pecan cake, 56
pepper biscuits, Swedish, 20
pistachio sablés, 36
preserves, 84–93
  cranberry and basil relish, 87
  ginger fruit relish, 88
  maple squash butter, 91
  red fruit conserve, 92

R
raisins:
  Christmas mini-muffins, 60
  cider fruit squares, 48
  ginger fruit relish, 88
red fruit conserve, 92
redcurrant jelly:
  red fruit conserve, 92

relishes:
  cranberry and basil relish, 87
  ginger fruit relish, 88
rosemary:
  marinated olives, 83
royal icing, 15

S
sablés:
  pistachio sablés, 36
  walnut sablés, 79
saffron cake, Swedish, 55
Sardinian almond biscuits, 28
sesame seeds:
  grissini, 80
spicy nuts, 83
squash:
  maple squash butter, 91
star biscuits, iced, 16
sterilizing jars, 4
sultanas:
  cider fruit squares, 48
Swedish pepper biscuits, 20

Swedish saffron cake, 55
sweets:
  chocolate and cream fudge,
    67
  Christmas truffles, 68

T
thyme:
  marinated olives, 83
triple chocolate brownies, 44
triple chocolate cookies, 27
truffles, Christmas, 68

V
vanilla butter biscuits, Dutch,
  23

W
walnuts:
  chocolate brandy cake, 52
  flourless sticky brownies, 47
  triple chocolate cookies, 27
  walnut sablés, 79